Craft Union

noun

Definition:

A union representing workers who share the same skill-set and passion or who perform similar tasks, although they may work in different industries; e.g. brewers and chefs.

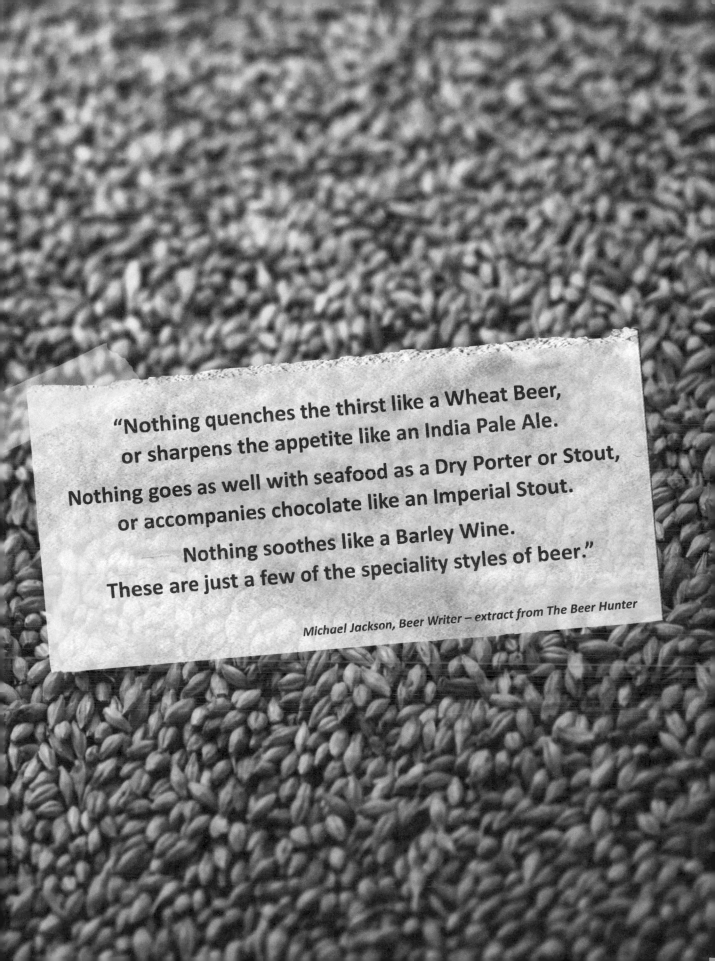

"Nothing quenches the thirst like a Wheat Beer,
or sharpens the appetite like an India Pale Ale.

Nothing goes as well with seafood as a Dry Porter or Stout,
or accompanies chocolate like an Imperial Stout.

Nothing soothes like a Barley Wine.
These are just a few of the speciality styles of beer."

Michael Jackson, Beer Writer – extract from The Beer Hunter

Contents

FOREWORD BY

PETE BROWN

I get the call while I'm on holiday in France – a well-earned break after the launch of my second book in summer 2006. A guy called Alex Buchanan is phoning from a brewery in the Peak District, asking if I'd be interested in doing an after-dinner speech for them.

I'm in no position to turn down a paying gig so I say yes. I have a reading scheduled as part of a literary festival in Sheffield and Alex suggests I come out to the brewery that evening and stay the night. I've been invited to visit lots of breweries, but I've never been asked to stay overnight before.

My reading is at the Fat Cat pub and my host is owner Dave Wickett, who sadly died prematurely in 2012. He's heavily jetlagged after returning from a visit to his cask ale pub in New York.

As he puts me into a cab at the end of the evening, he says something strange, which I attribute to the jetlag – at that stage anyway: "I'm so envious of you. You're just about to encounter Thornbridge for the first time. You lucky bastard."

No one else I know has heard of Thornbridge, so this comment is cryptic to say the least. But over the ensuing half-decade tens of thousands of craft beer fans will encounter a Thornbridge beer for the first time – and after they have done so, they will envy their friends who are about to have the same experience.

For some, the first sip of Thornbridge will be the first time they have tasted the new style of craft beer that's sweeping the world and making beer more exciting than it's been in living memory... The first time they've had their palates dazzled by the vivid fruity flavours of new world hops; the vinous, spirituous tease imparted by careful wood ageing; or the bold, muscular elegance of imperial stouts and porters. The first time you experience beers like this it's like tasting in colour and realising that you've only had black and white until now.

When I arrive at Thornbridge Hall, the bar in the old coach house next to the impressive stately home has just waved goodbye to a local CAMRA (Campaign for Real Ale) visit, so all the beers are on tap ready to go. There's an expectant air. I try to be cool and analytical like I think beer critics should be. But after two beers I say: "My God, this is what I've been talking about! This is what I've been looking for! How do you know about these flavours?"

The men and women from Thornbridge look pleasantly amused, kind and tolerant. Even in these early days I guess they get this reaction quite a lot.

Fast forward to 2009 and I'm staying at Thornbridge Hall again, having been invited to help brew Jaipur. For a beer writer this is like being invited to get up and jam on stage with your favourite band – though of course, all I'll be doing is what the brewers allow me to do, when they tell me.

It's just gone 8am as I walk through the dew-dropped gardens, past the risqué yet sombre statues that have begun appearing on Thornbridge's beer labels. As I draw closer to the old carpenter's shed the music of Joy Division grows louder. It's deafening by the time I get to the brewery. The anguished cries of the Manchester legends are serenading the fermenters from a laptop PC hooked up to beefy speakers.

I do the bits that beer writers normally do when invited to a brew day – tipping in a few sacks of malt, having my photo taken when we add the hops to the copper later. But in between I get more than I bargained for. I'm taken to a shed across the pathway that's been turned into a brewer's laboratory and given an intensive seminar on the subject of healthy yeast. Blue dye is added to a sample taken from a recent brew and I'm shown how to count healthy cells through a microscope and learn that when the number of healthy cells falls below a certain number the yeast needs to be refreshed.

And that's when I realise one of Thornbridge's secrets — only one, but a very important one — here the brewers share the passionate sense of adventure and experimentation that's now infecting young microbrewers across Britain. But they ally this to a rigour and discipline that the biggest brewers in the world would admire, especially in an operation so small. And then they throw in a dash of classic post-punk to fermentation, just to make sure.

Thornbridge Brewery started in 2004 after Jim Harrison, owner of Thornbridge Hall, and his business partner Simon Webster (cajoled by friend Dave Wickett who provided his experience as an established brewer), set up a small brewing operation in one of the Hall's small outbuildings.

At a time when many ales were very similar in colour, taste and strength, Thornbridge had set out its stall with an array of beers built around diversity and drinkability, where they believe the strength of a good beer lies. Jaipur, the intensely flavoured 5.9% IPA was joined by Lord Marples, a 4% take on a classic British bitter and Saint Petersburg, a 7.4% ABV inky, rich stout. Beer bloggers continued to do Thornbridge's marketing for them, spreading the word. And the constant stream of awards didn't do any harm. The accolades and publicity led to high levels of demand for their beers: "We could quite happily just brew Jaipur 24/7 and we'd still never be able to meet demand," said Simon Webster, "but that's not the brewery any of us want to work for."

It seems Thornbridge can do no wrong. What's their secret? The way Jim Harrison tells it, it's very simple. "If we want someone to do a particular job for us we always hire someone who is better at that job than we are."

The modest brewery in the old carpenter's shed couldn't cope any more. So a major financial investment saw the building of a new, state-of-the-art brewery at Riverside in Bakewell, a few miles from Thornbridge Hall. Within a year the new brewery was at capacity. The addition of new storage vessels then doubled that capacity. And within a year volumes had doubled again.

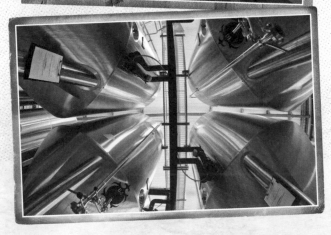

As literally hundreds of new microbreweries opened across the UK, enjoying the growing interest in craft beer, Thornbridge grew rapidly from microbrewery to significant regional player and even began exporting beers like Jaipur to the US, from where their inspiration originally came.

At the same time, the brewery was building up an exciting chain of pubs. In many of these, the food is as important as the beer. Richard Smith (who simply begs to be described as the man who put the 'chef' in Sheffield) partnered with Thornbridge at the Coach & Horses and then the Cricket Inn, which went from serving one cask beer pump to a range of Thornbridge ales that outsold everything else on the bar put together, and served up food that was recognisable as traditional pub fare but, just like the beers, took quality and flavour to another level.

The relationship with Smith is typical of a broader philosophy of collaboration. Thornbridge wants to learn from others, and share its own knowledge, and has done so with other leading brewers worldwide. As Thornbridge emerges on a national and even international stage, the people running it retain the energy and enthusiasm of a new start-up. And they just seem to have so much damn fun doing what they do.

Fast forward again to 2011. I'm standing in the control room at the Riverside Brewery, gazing out over ranks of stainless steel vessels. Long gone are the days when brewers (and bloggers) had to climb into the copper with a hose to clean it down from the inside – here, everything is automated. Rather than dumbing down the job, this removal of manual labour has freed up time for the brewers to experiment and be creative, and if anyone really does feel like getting their hands dirty, the old brewery is still there in the carpenter's shed, a test plant producing the specialist Thornbridge Hall range of more esoteric beers.

Down here, they're finishing a 'double IPA' – a sort of beefed-up distant cousin of Jaipur. It's been designed by Dom Driscoll, who joined recently from Manchester brewery Marble, and Matthew Clark, one of the longest standing brewers here. The brewery has always been bigger than any one person – an idea and a philosophy that draws a steady stream of people to it. Caolan Vaughan has joined as lead brewer from Little Creatures in Australia, and Rob Lovatt as brewery manager from Meantime in London. The band of brewers is always evolving but the ethos stays the same.

"These guys have brewed more beer than Thornbridge ever has," says Simon, "They're the next chapter in our growth."

With new influences shaping this brewing schedule, Thornbridge has begun exploring craft keg ales and different lager styles, at the same time as constantly building expertise in getting more consistency into cask ales.

Incredibly, this is the first time Thornbridge has made a double IPA. It's always been on the list, but there's never been a gap in the schedule. I get a taste from the fermenter. There's a sweaty, piney smell that causes a Pavlovian reaction, making me anticipate a flavour explosion. When it comes it's lychee and peach and a hint of banana with a smooth, succulent mouth-feel. Very balanced, sweet and mouth-wateringly fruity then a slow-building dry tingle. It's 8.5% and drinks like 5.5%. Thornbridge has always made classy beers, never extreme or shocking for the sake of it.

So what's next? The keg beers are opening up new markets and new potential. And in the world of craft beer, there'll always be something new to explore. This brewery is a learning environment for anyone who is passionate about beer, a place where hard work feels like play.

"There's no exit strategy for us," muses Simon, "We want to see our children working here one day. We like to think of ourselves as a first generation family brewer."

It takes an effort of will to resist asking if they'll adopt me.

— Pete Brown
award-winning beer writer

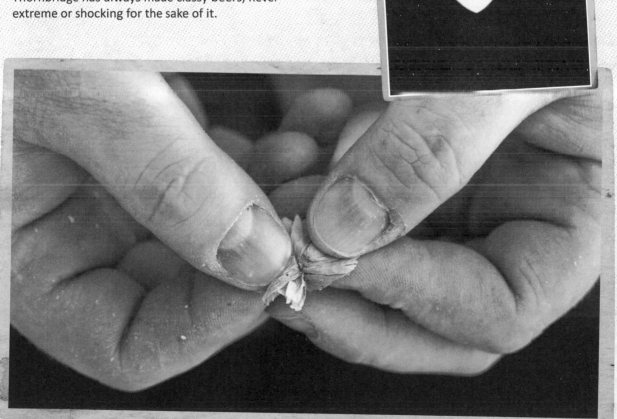

A GUIDE TO BEER & FOOD MATCHING
BY ALEX BARLOW

We love beer and we love food, and matching them is something our customers do every day in many of our pubs and restaurants.

A lot has been written about pairing the two, but there is boundless diversity and intricacy and there are no hard and fast rules. We wanted to produce a guide, not a rule book in order to share our thoughts and knowledge with people eager to learn more about how they can be paired together.

Our main ethos is to have fun – something our friend and Master Brewer Alex Barlow agrees with. So we asked him for his expert advice on the subject of how to get the best from beer and food.

– Alex Barlow

www.allbeerfinder.com
@allbeerfinder

World of Choice

In all respects, beer is the most natural partner for food. It is the most widely drunk alcoholic beverage across all continents with a diversity of flavour unmatched by any other drink, alcoholic or not. From light and crisp to richly rounded; bitter grapefruit, savoury or tropically-sweet; roast chocolate or coffee – beer can do it all. However, it is conspicuous by its absence when we're considering what to drink with our meal.

Why is this?

Popular cultural perception seems to equate food with wine. This may be due to concerted campaigns by the wine industry to educate supermarket buyers and their customers, but the rise in demand for wine coincided with beer's darkest times in terms of quality and choice here in the UK.

Now things are very different. There has never been such an exciting selection of quality craft-brewed

domestic and imported beer. The choice is superb and seems to grow by the week. Although there's admittedly still work to do in providing information to help people make informed choices that suit their tastes and that make the ideal partner for their food.

So, here goes. The following section is intended to whet your appetite: an introduction to some of the most popular beer styles, the types of flavours they exhibit and a simple guide for how to match them with your chosen foods.

The most important thing is to have fun trying. There is no definitive right and wrong in flavour matching, as long as it works for you. So enjoy!

For a wide selection of beer and food choices, including Thornbridge Brewery beers, take a look at www.allbeerfinder.com.

Bringing it together: simple guidelines to help your selections:

CLEANSE:

Beers refresh the palate between mouthfuls. They generally have less alcohol and body than wines and provide a quenching mouthful, whether with spicy and salty snacks or rich chocolate cake. Carbonation physically cleanses the palate, while bitterness and mild acidity help lift fats.

COORDINATE:

Match lighter flavoured beers with lighter foods to ramp up the flavours in both (look for 'flavour intensity' ratings on allbeerfinder.com). Remember that colour doesn't define flavour intensity: some pilsners or American pale ales can be quite challenging while dark lager or mild can be more subtle.

COMPLEMENT:

Selecting beers with characteristics similar to those in the food ensure a harmony and blending of flavours. This provides a background for other flavour features to be expressed. For example, the herbal hops of a pilsner work superbly with those in a pizza.

CONTRAST:

With particularly strongly flavoured foods, a beer expressing some contrasting character can create overall balance in the meal. For example, a clean and crisp, light lager to accompany sticky sweet and sour sauce, or a classic British bitter with sticky toffee pudding.

Style: Bitter & Pale Ale

Background:
More bitter than traditional milds, the popular, staple beers of British family and craft brewers.

Typical flavours:
Refreshing blends of biscuit and light roasted malts balanced by floral grassy or earthy hops, subtle fruits with a quenching dry, bitter finish.

Partner with:
Sausages and pork pies; roast pork, lamb or beef; mushrooms; medium cheddar; fruit crumble or sticky toffee pudding.

Style: Pilsner

Background:
Originating in Czech Republic in 1842, the first truly golden lager beer created a style popularised across Europe and worldwide.

Typical flavours:
Czech pilsner is full and smooth, with buttery malts and firm balancing bitterness. Continental pilsners tend to be more crisp and herbal.

Partner with:
Spit-roast or chicken schnitzel; cured pork, ham and sausages; herby pizza or pasta; nutty Emmental and smoked cheeses.

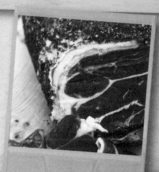

Style: Gueuze

Background:
First appearing in the 19th century, gueuze is a blend of young and older spontaneously-fermented lambics, which create a more lively carbonated beer. Easier to drink than oude lambic beers.

Typical flavours:
Zingy sweet and sour character with little, if any, bitterness. Light honeyed malts, maybe some vanilla and just a hint of cheesy or goaty farmyard aroma.

Partner with:
Superb as a cleansing aperitif or between courses. Great with mussels, crab, sardines and mackerel; blue brie or Danish blue; cheesecake.

Style: IPA (India Pale Ale)

Background:
The strongest, most highly-hopped of pale ales, originally brewed to withstand the long sea voyage to India. Often use New World hops.

Typical flavours:
Robust beers with a boat-load of malt, fruit & floral aromas. Full and rounded, balancing high levels of spicy bitterness and a dry finish.

Partner with:
Match the spice of Indian curries; Cajun BBQ and burgers with chilli relish; Shropshire Blue cheese; creamy fruit Pavlova.

Style: Light Lager

Background:
Originating in US, and across Asia. Based on pilsner but use rice or maize to dilute malt flavour, with low hop addition rates.

Typical flavours:
Served extra cold for maximum refreshment. Clean and light with high carbonation and low bitterness and aftertaste.

Partner with:
Salty snacks and tortillas; pasta and salads; white fish and tuna; brie or cottage cheese; tropical fruit; milk chocolate.

Style: Fruit Beers

Background:
Traditionally based on brown ale or lambic gueuze but taking the flavour and colour of the cherry, raspberry or other fruit they are matured with.

Typical flavours:
Rich fruit aromas and colour. Lambic-based beers are thinner, sharper and more acidic in nature while ale bases are more sweet, malty and rounded.

Partner with:
The obvious match is with fruit desserts, but can complement or contrast with roast game birds and meats; chocolate desserts or petit fours.

Style: Porter & Stout

Background:
Originating in 18th century London, porter and stout use copious amounts of dark roast malts for a near black body. Usually not too hoppy.

Typical flavours:
Espresso-dark, intensely roasted, full-bodied and full-flavoured. May be sweet or more sharp, with a long bitter coffee or chocolate finish.

Partner with:
Sweet and salty shellfish; beef or game casserole; Cheshire or Wensleydale cheese; tiramisu and rich chocolate desserts.

Style: Dark Lager

Background:
The way all lager was before Pilsner Urquell came along in 1842. From dark amber to near black in colour and highly carbonated.

Typical flavours:
Dark colours belie surprisingly smooth and clean beer, with toasted nut and roast character, gentle bitter-sweet balance and a light, dry finish.

Partner with:
Perfect with blackened salmon; Cajun chicken or fish; Mexican beef dishes; German wurst; mushrooms, mild cheeses; caramel or coffee desserts.

Style: Barley Wine, Dubbel & Triple

Background:
Strong British or Belgian-style beers, double or triple fermented to achieve 8-12% alcohol – so go steady!

Typical flavours:
Triple & barley wines are generally pale, while Dubbel darker. Intense alcohol warmth, rich fruits, blended with peppery hops and strong sweet malts.

Partner with:
Richly refined tastes suit game birds, darker beers with game meats; charcuterie; fruit compotes; crème brulee; nuts; a good cheese board.

Style: Blonde

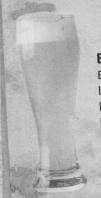

Typical flavours:
Refreshing, easy drinking beers, light in colour, medium body with fruity aromas and a sweet tangy finish.

Background:
Brewed with pale or lager malts, the ale brewers' answer to big brand lagers.

Partner with:
Prawns; fish and chips; poultry salad or terrines; ham and bacon; apricot Stilton; French-style fruit tarts.

Style: Bock

Typical flavours:
May be light or dark, with rich bready malts, full-on alcohol warmth and a background of peppery, spicy hops.

Background:
Means 'goat' in German and often features one on the label. Bock is like lager pumped on steroids.

Partner with:
Suits strong-flavoured game, liver or kidneys; bacon; duck; Mexican beans; nuts; gruyere; cherries.

Style: Wheat Beers

Typical flavours:
Range from near white, citrusy and spicy Witte beers to amber or dark brown dunkel Weizen, with banana, apple and clove-like aromas.

Background:
Belgian Witte (white) or Bavarian Weizen (wheat) styles use 30-50% wheat malt for a lighter body and taste, usually cloudy and unfiltered.

Partner with:
Witte are excellent with mussels and white fish or lighter Thai or Chinese dishes while Weizen suit smoked haddock, trout or salmon; apple strudel; Bavarian cheese.

WHERE IT ALL BEGAN
THE HISTORY OF THORNBRIDGE BREWERY

A brief history of Thornbridge Brewery

Thornbridge is an award-winning brewery, nestled in the inspirational landscape of the Peak District National Park, Derbyshire.

Producing around 100,000 pints of beer a week and having won hundreds of awards, the brewery has quickly become a well-respected player in the British brewing industry. Perhaps surprising to note, then, that this was never quite the plan...

2004 was drawing to a close and business partners Jim Harrison and Simon Webster were looking for a beer to add to a range of Thornbridge branded products, so named after Jim's home – stately Thornbridge Hall at Ashford-In-The-Water.

With no intention to brew it themselves, Jim and Simon approached Sheffield beer expert and founder of Kelham Island Brewery, the late Dave Wickett, only to find themselves amicably rebuffed. Instead, Dave suggested they set up their own operation.

Thornbridge Hall

Thornbridge Hall provided the ideal location. Built and maintained as the seat of the Longsdon family from the 12th to 18th century, it has continued to see successive ownership and redevelopment. The Hall was enlarged by the Morewood family, who lived at Thornbridge from 1790, but perhaps its first big change came when Frederick Craven moved in in 1859 and rebuilt the house in the Victorian style.

Thirty-seven years later, George Jobson Marples, a businessman and barrister from nearby Sheffield, made the second big change when he enlarged the house again in mock-Jacobean style. His grand redevelopment included extending the hall with an extra storey, building lodges and cottages within the grounds, as well as landscaping the park and gardens, adding his own private railway station and acquiring the Watson buffet fountain from nearby Chatsworth.

Other major additions were made in subsequent years. Sheffield entrepreneur Charles Boot added fireplaces, marble columns and garden statuary from, amongst others, Clumber House, and panelling from Derwent Hall around 1929. Wood from old churches dating back to the 1650s and wooden carvings from around 1590 have also been added, although their origins are undocumented.

Between 1945 and 1997, the Hall ceased to be a residence when Sheffield City Council ran the site as an educational training centre.

Restoration work to the gardens and removal of ill-fitting additions to the house were started by the Hunt family in 1997 and the building's true proportions were finally revealed. Owned by Jim and Emma Harrison since 2002, Thornbridge Hall now leads a dual existence, as both a private family home and an exclusive venue for events and weddings.

While brewing was commonplace at many of England's country estates, there is no evidence that Thornbridge ever housed its own operation. So it was George Marples' outbuildings that provided the potential for Jim and Simon to create their country house brewery.

Setting up

Not the types to shy away from a challenge, Jim and Simon laid their hands on second-hand equipment from a brewery that was closing down and set up in an old stone mason's workshop in the Thornbridge Hall grounds.

Equipment they could do – brewing, they couldn't.

Enter two young, enthusiastic brewers: Italian food scientist Stefano Cossi and Scottish brewing graduate Martin Dickie. Fresh out of training and keen to channel their creative energies, the duo set to work. After months of research and experimentation, they created one of Thornbridge's now staple beers: a classic 4% bitter, Lord Marples, in homage to the Hall's previous owner.

The big breakthrough

The big breakthrough came in June 2005 with the evolution of what is arguably Thornbridge's most famous beer, Jaipur – a 5.9% hoppy India Pale Ale.

September of the same year saw Jaipur pick up honours at the Sheffield CAMRA Awards, which was the catalyst for a whole host of accolades, resulting in more and more demand from pubs to stock Thornbridge beers.

Jaipur has since gone on to win countless awards, including Brewing Industry International Best Keg Ale, and has been named in the UK's top 50 food and drink products by the Guild of Fine Foods. Following this it went on to win the regionals, making it one of the top 10 food and drink products in the UK.

Sensing that this was no longer an expensive hobby, Jim and Simon took steps to grow the brewery and took on marketing manager Alex Buchanan – as a van driver. For Alex, driving a van around the Peak District making beer deliveries to small pubs was a relaxing way to get away from the more corporate working background he'd been used to. Little did he know that it wouldn't last for long...

Expansion continued so rapidly that the workforce simply couldn't keep up with demand and two more brewers were brought on board.

It was also at this time that Jim and Simon realised they had another big decision to make – remain a small ten-barrel plant producing 200 nine-gallon casks over five brews a week, or start looking at developing the business further. The latter won out and the business partners started looking for the ideal location for their brewery.

Inspired by the Peak District

There was no question that the new building would operate from the National Park, which began and continues to provide inspiration to the brewers and staff. A little bit of this unspoilt paradise goes into every bottle of beer – Thornbridge's way of giving people the chance to enjoy a product of the beautiful Peak District.

Settling on Bakewell's Riverside Business Park, a stone's throw from the Hall, they commissioned and built the £2million state-of-the-art brewery which opened at the beginning of September 2009.

The business continued to expand rapidly with yet more awards coming their way and an exclusive deal seeing Thornbridge beers stocked nationwide in supermarket Waitrose.

Thornbridge's big sellers, such as Jaipur, Lord Marples and Wild Swan, are brewed at the Riverside on a daily basis, while the smaller Hall brewery is used for more bespoke runs, such as the 10% Bracia, infused with Italian chestnut honey. It also gives the brewers an outlet to experiment and let loose their creative energies.

With 2012 drawing to a close, Thornbridge is now making its mark on the global market. Around 25 per cent of its beer is exported to countries including America, Sweden, Canada, Finland, Romania, Spain, Italy, Poland, Australia and India – and that number continues to rise with new launches taking place all the time.

THE BIRTH OF
BREWKITCHEN

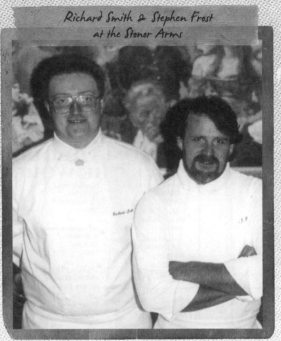

Richard Smith & Stephen Frost
at the Stonor Arms

With beer comes food...

Like many conversations, it all started in a pub...

The friendship between Jim Harrison, award-winning Sheffield chef Richard Smith and his wife Victoria was forged back in 1995. The Smiths had opened their first restaurant in the Steel City, Smith's, where the Harrisons became regular diners.

Simon Webster also knew the Smiths during his time as marketing director at Henderson's Relish – a favourite ingredient of the Smiths that they'd taken round the world on their culinary travels.

Richard began stocking Thornbridge beers at the restaurant and became more involved with Thornbridge when they approached him to design and deliver a menu for a brewery dinner at the Hall. For Thornbridge, it was a case of putting beer at the level of a chef at the top of his game, pairing quality with quality and harking back to Jim's ethos of always employing someone better than you to do the job.

When Jim and Simon opened the brewery together, a natural progression was to have their own pubs – and with pubs come food. After Richard's brewery dinner went down a storm, he was top of their list of people to approach, and with Victoria's front-of-house expertise it was a match made in, um, a pub.

Don't mention the 'G' word...

Richard's background lies firmly in 'gastropubs' – a term now banned by The Good Food Guide on the grounds that it has lost its meaning as growing numbers of landlords offer food alongside the traditional pint and packet of crisps.

However, it was back in the '80s, at 'gastropub' the Stonor Arms in Henley on Thames, that Richard first honed his craft under his mentor – Master Chef of Great Britain Stephen Frost. Richard found inspiration in abundance, both at work and watching what other chefs were doing.

"Apart from Stephen Frost, in my mind, there are three 'founding fathers' of great British food in pubs, all of whom I've spent some time with," says Richard. "There's my namesake, Richard Smith, of the Royal Oak, Yattendon, who took great Mayfair cuisine and put high restaurant quality into pubs for the first time.

"Then Franco Taruschio of The Walnut Tree at Abergavenny. He brought an odd mix of rustic Welsh and Italian food, but it was finely tuned and attracted customers from all over the country.

"Finally, over in north Yorkshire, Denis Watkins was cooking classical British at the Angel Inn at Hetton. He also had a great love of wine and was instrumental in bringing good quality wine to the pub."

Richard feels that country pubs started this 'revolution' of serving restaurant-quality cuisine; publicans realised people wanted better food and started taking on development chefs.

The concept took longer to hit London as it was already full of restaurants and bistros. Fast forward a few years and The Eagle on Farringdon Road became popular with artists, designers and journalists from nearby publishers. They were instrumental in bringing good food in pubs into city centres.

Richard's interest was also sparked by chefs Simon Hopkinson, co-founder of London's Bibendum, George Perry-Smith, founder of Bath's Hole in the Wall, Joyce Molyneux, Elizabeth David and Shaun Hill, who did things nobody else was doing in the UK at the time.

"At the Stonor Arms we were doing similar things that are still popular now and that we've carried through in BrewKitchen restaurants – it's where I got my values from. Our food ethos was to source the best ingredients possible then buy, cook and sell the same day, which meant our menus changed that frequently too depending on season and availability.

"We employed nose-to-tail cooking, buying a whole duck from the market and using the breast for the restaurant and legs for the bar. We were even matching food with beer back then and we'd source it from local breweries like Chiltern.

"We encouraged the community to get involved with supplying produce – our pot washer's mum made a soft cheese that we'd use in dishes that came to be known as Stonor Cheese, we foraged – all things that are back 'in trend' now. We didn't realise that it was all a precursor to what's happening now."

They were visited by chefs of modern 'celebrity', such as Raymond Blanc and John Burton-Race and superstars of the day including Deep Purple, Abba, Rowan Atkinson, Michael Heseltine, Sheffield's Marti Caine... even Prince Charles.

"Stephen Frost always talked about pubs being somewhere everyone was welcome – they are to Britain what bistros are to France and cafés are to Italy – and we proved it. It has remained part of my philosophy and hopefully that comes across in all our restaurants. I was fortunate enough to be there for three years and it was truly a dream job – it's the best job I ever had." says Richard.

"My experiences have convinced me that there are two styles of pub: those led by drink and community and those led by food. Thornbridge taps and BrewKitchen pubs and restaurants fit both bills."

The birth of BrewKitchen...

Richard's passion and enthusiasm left him with an ambition to own places of his own. And with the Thornbridge partnership in place, BrewKitchen began to grow.

It now boasts a plethora of pubs and restaurants in and around Sheffield, including Artisan, The Beauchief Restaurant & Rooms, The Cricket Inn, Graze Inn, The Inn at Troway, Thyme Café, Relish and the Rose Garden Café.

BrewKitchen restaurants don't aim to dictate what should and shouldn't go with food, but instead try to show the breadth of the possibilities.

"The partnership with Thornbridge works because we have a similar mindset and the same vision," says Richard. "We're in it for the long term and have no agendas. We want to employ people, make customers happy and look after establishments. If we don't, we've failed them."

THE GREAT COLCHESTER
OYSTER HUNT

Oh we do like to be beside the seaside...

Oysters, the infamous aphrodisiac, are customarily linked with fine Champagne or a crisp Sauvignon Blanc. But we like turning things on their head and there is nothing better than pairing them with the right beer.

However, even the best-laid plans can quickly come apart at the seams if one element goes slightly awry...

Our day in Colchester had one focus: to source and cook with its most famous export – native oysters. The seaside town's combination of warm, muddy water, plankton and algae have created the perfect conditions for oysters to thrive and be sought the world over since Roman times.

We were desperate to get our hands on some –

but acquisition is a different story altogether. Almost two million native oysters are harvested in Colchester every year, but such is the demand that most are spoken for long before they're prised from their watery beds. Trying to source a few at the end of the season in April? Only a madman would waste a second on such a wild goose chase.

Good job we're a bit of a mad bunch, then.

After a 4am start from Sheffield, our intrepid group – expert chefs Richard Smith and Jack Baker, photographer Jodi Hinds, my colleague Caolan and I – had almost lost hope of finding any oysters, meeting rejection from bemused fishmongers at every turn. I've never been laughed at with such disdain so many times in one day!

Trying to remain optimistic, we dusted ourselves down and re-thought our plans. The chefs purchased a range of fresh fish to cook regardless of our oyster disappointment: seabass, sole, scallops, prawns, hake, cockles and mussels. The sun was shining and we weren't about to waste our journey, nor the mobile larder we'd created in the back of our van. Jack's family had kindly lent us their beach hut at Mersea Island and let's face it; the beer wasn't going to drink itself. But as we boys prepared to drown our sorrows, the female member of the expedition came up trumps...

Kudos goes to Jodi, who disappeared to put her initiative (and supreme blagging skills) to good use. She returned with a handful of native oysters from the extremely kind folk at The Company Shed – one of Colchester's biggest oyster exporters.

Disaster and heartbreak averted, we had everything we needed and more for our seaside pop-up kitchen.

We even discovered that the local Mersea Island Brewery had created Oyster Ale, a 5% ABV ale combining oats, light and dark malts and a small measure of Fuggles hops.

According to the brewers, each cask has eight oysters added to it, giving one pint in eight the chance of expressing the aphrodisiac properties of the shellfish. I have always maintained the opinion that beer is sexy.

Beer and fish purchased, the chefs rustled up some of the finest food I've ever tasted. Smithy always tells me one of his most memorable meals was eating freshly-caught crab, sitting on the river banks at Chesapeake Bay in Maryland, USA. I was always jealous of that story but now I was experiencing the same: eating fresh oysters and fish, sitting on the beach just yards from where they had earlier been caught – plus I had some great beers to go with them.

The sun shone very brightly that day and all of us who were there will never forget the experience that good food and beer brought us.

– Simon Webster

COLCHESTER OYSTERS

Colchester native oysters develop in the Pyefleet Creek and Colne Estuary, maturing for four to five years before being harvested between the months of September to April.

Rock oysters are matured in the layings of the Pyefleet Creek and reach a prime size after two years. They are harvested throughout the year.

Oysters with shallot vinegar Serves 2

Ingredients

12 native Colchester oysters, shucked (opened)

30g shallots, finely chopped

55ml red wine vinegar

1 small bottle Tabasco

1 lemon wedge

Method

Make sure all the excess shell from the shucked oysters is discarded

In a small ramekin mix the shallots with the red wine vinegar

Present the oysters on a bed of ice, on a board or plate. Garnish with the shallot vinegar, Tabasco and lemon

What we drank ...

Guinness and oysters is a classic combination, with a match in smooth texture and saltiness. We felt Thornbridge Tzara made a pleasantly refreshing pairing, with a subtle sweetness that matches the oysters yet cleanses the acidity and chilli.

Pan-fried line caught rockfish with avocado compote, tomato salsa, lemon & olive oil Serves 4

Ingredients

Fish

4 170g rockfish (ask your fishmonger to scale and pin-bone)

Olive oil

Roquette

Tomato Salsa

115g vine tomatoes, deseeded and diced

30g red onions, finely diced

30g green pepper, finely diced

30g red pepper, finely diced

30g yellow pepper, finely diced

15g spring onions, finely shredded

Pinch of freshly chopped red chillies

1 lime, juiced and zested

1 orange, juiced and zested

1 tablespoon fresh coriander, chopped

Pinch of ground cumin

Salt and pepper

Lemon Oil

100ml olive oil

1 lemon, zested

1 teaspoon salt

Avocado Compote

85g avocado, diced

85g avocado, mashed

Henderson's Relish

Tabasco

1 tablespoon coriander, chopped

1 lime, juiced and zested

1 tablespoon basil, finely shredded

Olive oil

Salt and pepper

Method

Fish

Put a drizzle of olive oil into a non-stick pan

Season the rockfish with sea salt and freshly cracked pepper

When the pan is hot, sear the fish for two minutes on each side

Add a knob of butter and put to one side to rest

To serve, put some of the tomato salsa in the centre of a plate. Place the fish on top, then a good dollop of avocado salsa. Drizzle with lemon and chive oil and add a few sprigs of roquette

Tomato Salsa

Place all the ingredients in a bowl, mix and season to taste

Lemon Oil

Heat the olive oil in a small pan to a medium heat and then add the fresh lemon peel and salt. Allow to cool then add the chives

Avocado Compote

Place all the ingredients in a bowl, mix gently and season to taste

What we drank ...

The delicate sweetness and firm texture of the rockfish demands a pale beer with good fruity flavours and a bit of bite to match the complexity and spicy zing of the compote and salsa. We thought both Thornbridge Jaipur and Little Creatures Pale Ale worked perfectly.

Seafood vongole with clams, scallops, crab & rockfish

Serves 2

Ingredients

Large handful fresh clams

6 large scallops

115g crab meat

Lemon juice

4 60g pieces of rockfish

60g shallots, finely diced

2 cloves garlic, finely diced

2 sprigs fresh thyme

200ml Thornbridge Jaipur beer

60g tomato concasse (peeled and diced)

1 teaspoon fresh basil, shredded

1 teaspoon red chilli, finely diced

1 tablespoon parsley, finely shredded

400g cooked spaghetti

Fresh parmesan

What we drank ...

Using a pale but flavoursome beer like Thornbridge Jaipur or Duvel in the reduction ensures you can serve the same with it too, while we thought the smooth, citrusy bite of Thornbridge Wild Swan went perfectly.

Method

In a hot pan add a dash of olive oil, then add the clams and toss around with the lid on for 30 seconds

Add the shallots, garlic, thyme, Thornbridge Jaipur beer and finely diced red chilli

Reduce the stock down for a couple of minutes and add the scallops, crab and rockfish. Cook for a further minute

Add the cooked spaghetti, tomato, basil, parsley and a squeeze of lemon juice

Serve in pasta bowls, garnished with freshly grated parmesan

Top Tip

Any selection of seafood can be used for this dish. A good tip is to choose whatever is freshly available that you enjoy. Mussels, langoustines, lobster, monkfish, hake and jumbo king prawns work really well. Delicious!

Spicy avocado & local Colchester crab salad Serves 2

Ingredients

Salad

115g crab meat

30g red onion, finely sliced

115g avocado, diced

60g cherry tomatoes, halved

1 tablespoon dill, roughly chopped

Wedge of lime

2 sprigs parsley

Selection of salad leaves

Dressing

1 tablespoon balsamic vinegar

3 tablespoons olive oil

1 teaspoon wholegrain mustard

Method

Place all the salad ingredients into a large mixing bowl, saving a third of the crab for the garnish. Lightly season with sea salt and crushed black pepper

In a separate bowl, make a quick and easy vinaigrette with the dressing ingredients. Simply whisk together the vinegar and mustard and slowly add the olive oil

Toss two thirds of the vinaigrette through the salad ingredients and split the salad between the two bowls

Top the salad with the extra leftover crab and drizzle with the leftover vinaigrette

Garnish with parsley and fresh Thornbridge beer bread, drizzled with olive oil

Top Tip

If crab isn't available this great, simple salad works well with lobster too

What we drank ...

The invigorating carbonation and fresh nuttiness of Schneider Weisse Tap 7 Original was perfect with the avocado and crab.

Thornbridge Versa with similar characteristics works equally well.

Creamy Thornbridge Kipling ale fish stew Serves 2

Ingredients

60g sole fillets

60g rockfish fillets (local white flesh fish, native to the Colchester area)

2 sprigs thyme

2 garlic cloves, finely diced

50g shallots, finely diced

2 bay leaves

150ml Thornbridge Kipling ale

1 large handful clams

85g crab meat, white and brown

6 scallops, out of shell with the roe on

1 teaspoon dill, finely chopped

1 tablespoon parsley, chopped

300ml double cream

30g tomato concasse (skinned and de-seeded)

Method

To a hot pan drizzle a dash of olive oil. Add the clams, thyme, garlic, shallots, bay leaves and Kipling ale. Lightly season with sea salt and white pepper

Reduce the liquid to a third and then add the cream, scallops, rockfish and crab

Simmer for two minutes until the fish is cooked through. Add the parsley, dill and tomato concasse

Add seasoning to taste and serve with fresh home-baked bread and lemon wedges

What we drank ...

Thornbridge Kipling is an obvious partner as it features in the dish and has a sweetness that matches the scallops and crab with a fruity bite that contrasts and refreshes. Pure Gold from Purity works very nicely too.

THE
CRICKET INN

A year-round family affair...

Pubs have always been extremely close to my heart – Sheffield's Cricket Inn especially so. During my childhood it was run by my grandfather's cousin, making it a big part of my heritage, so I was delighted when it became part of our group.

My grandfather himself ran the Crown Inn just down the road, meaning I spent a lot of my former years in the family pubs and have some fond memories. I loved visiting them after school, drowning bags of crisps in Henderson's Relish and shaking them up to coat them for flavour. The challenge was to eat them before they went soggy. And we all remember the day we get to sip our first pint...

Personal attachment aside, what I love about the Cricket Inn is that it's a little oasis for Sheffield and the Peak District, with quintessentially English pub elements enhancing its character throughout the year.

The rolling fields behind are magical in the warmer months. I've spent many a happy hour sitting outside with friends and family, nursing a cold beer while watching a game of cricket on the pitch out the back. Kids and dogs bound around your feet, chargrilled barbecue smells waft on the breeze and the sun shines. It's a beautiful location.

The Cricket in winter is equally spectacular. Roaring log fires, laughter, comforting food and cosy

nooks and crannies make it a home from home. The staff are like an extended family, always there to offer recommendations and look after your every whim, and the stream of regulars is testament to this. It's a proper pub, pure and simple.

The focus on seasonal menus reflects these elements too and gives our chefs freedom to experiment and satisfy their curiosity without restriction. In my mind, a fundamental part of any pub is that anyone and everyone should be welcome. The sign above the door to the Cricket reads 'Muddy boots, children and dogs welcome', which is as it should be.

The pub maintains the standards that I've held as important since my career began – we do things properly and we don't scrimp on quality, which I'm proud of.

All that taken into consideration, there was nowhere better to spend a glorious day for this chapter of the book. Our group chef, Les Rennie,

who held a Michelin star back in the day, teamed up with the Cricket's head chef Marco Caires to lay on a barbecue fit for a king.

Alongside our regulars, many staff from the Thornbridge and BrewKitchen families came along to join in (kids and dogs included). We made a lot of memories that day and having them on the page in the book makes them even more special.

I think the photos speak for themselves in this chapter – hopefully the fun we had comes across. But our Cricket barbecues are legendary, so if you don't believe me then pop along one summer and see for yourself.

– Richard Smith

THE 'BOOK' PUB

Our fondness for the Cricket Inn made it an obvious place to feature in a chapter of Craft Union. Some brilliant memories were made that day, which were captured beautifully in Jodi's photographs.

We wanted to share the fun we had with as many people as possible and show off what a fantastic destination pub the Cricket really is. Next time you're in have a wander round the rooms and look at the pictures framed on the walls – you'll see some from the book you recognise, and some you don't.

BBQ seabass Serves 4

Ingredients

4 450g whole seabass, gutted, scaled and washed

4 banana leaves (we grow our own red leaves, but vine leaves can be used as an alternative)

2 lemons, halved

Marinade

200ml extra virgin olive oil

5g crushed black peppercorns

1 lemon, juiced and zested

2 cloves garlic, grated

2 sprigs thyme

2 sprigs rosemary

1 bay leaf

What we drank ...

We enjoyed the seabass with Thornbridge Tzara. The bready notes and fruity palate worked perfectly with the marinade. It would also go well with the citrus and spice notes of Vedette White.

Method

For the marinade

Roughly mix the herbs in a pestle and mortar then add the garlic, pepper and lemon zest

Pour the marinade into a container big enough to lie the four prepped fish in and put to one side

For the fish

Check that there are no scales left on the fish – if any remain, remove them using the back of a knife

Trim all the fins from the fish including the tail (your fishmonger can do this for you)

Pour on the oil and lemon juice

Make five deep cuts into each side of the fish at an angle. Place them in the dish with the marinade, spoon some over and rub it in

Cover with cling film and leave in the fridge for 4-6 hours before cooking

Half way through the marinade time turn the fish over

Take the fish out of the marinade, wrap in banana leaves and secure with skewers

Place on the BBQ, cook slowly in a corner and keep turning them. At the same time place the four halved lemons on the BBQ and colour them

To serve, gently remove the leaves from the fish and serve with the lemon and your choice of salad or vegetables

Top Tip

Colouring the lemons on the BBQ makes them easier to squeeze

The Cricket Inn steak burger with battered onion rings

Serves 6

Ingredients

Steak Burgers

1kg minced rump steak

Salt and pepper

2 ripe beef tomatoes, sliced

6 gherkins, halved

6 slices cheddar cheese

6 rashers streaky bacon

18 little gem lettuce leaves

6 good quality burger buns

Mayonnaise (to coat the buns)

Battered Onion Rings

Half a pint of batter (for recipe see fish and chip page)

100g flour, seasoned with 1 teaspoon salt and 1 teaspoon pepper

1 whole red onion, peeled

What we drank ...

This was a perfect match with Thornbridge Kill Your Darlings. Its toasted malts were great with the BBQ burger and bun, but was crisp and refreshing with the bacon and cheddar. You might also enjoy Maverick from Fyne Ales.

Method

For the burgers

Put the mince in a bowl and add the salt and pepper, then mix together using your hands

Split the mince into six and mould the burgers – they can be as thick as you like

Start to cook the burger and the bacon on a BBQ or in a skillet on a high heat to sear for about 3 minutes on each side. Finish in the oven for about 4 minutes or until cooked as desired

Slice the burger buns in half and chargrill or toast

Lay them flat on a work top and spread with mayonnaise

Add a little gem leaf, a halved gherkin, slices of tomato and season

Place the burgers in the buns with bacon and cheddar cheese on top

For the onion rings

Set the deep fat fryer to 180°c

Slice the red onions to 1 centimetre thick and drop into seasoned flour

Shake the excess flour from the onions and add to the batter one by one

Remove and shake off excess batter, then deep fry until golden, flipping half way through

Serve in the burger or on the side – it's up to you!

Top Tips

Chargrilling the burgers will give them extra taste

If onion rings aren't for you then sautéed or raw red onions work well too

Half BBQ chicken with chorizo, lemon & thyme Serves 4

Ingredients

Chickens

2 whole chickens

Small bunch fresh lemon thyme

250ml good quality olive oil

2 lemons, juiced and sliced 1cm thick

Salt and cracked black pepper

Chorizo

8cm cooking chorizo sausage, sliced 1cm thick

3 cloves garlic, crushed

50ml olive oil

1 sprig thyme

What we drank ...

We thought the aromatic piney hops and balanced bitterness of Thornbridge Halcyon was the perfect match for the spicy chorizo chicken, or you could try the real pine notes of Alba, Scots Pine Ale.

Method

This recipe requires time to marinade the chicken

Chickens

Place the chickens on a chopping board

With the skin side facing towards you, cut half way through the knuckle joint

Make two or three score marks through each of the legs

Flip the chicken over and cut through the drumstick joint

Lay the chickens in a container (a Tupperware or bowl would be fine)

Scrunch the thyme to release the flavour and add to the chicken with the rest of the ingredients

Gently rub the oil and seasoning into the cuts and massage for 4-5 minutes to get the flavours working

Place cling film over the container and marinate for 12 hours in the fridge

To cook the chickens on the BBQ start them very slowly in the coolest area. Keep turning them – they will take a while to cook through, but will be juicy and tender

Chorizo

Put all the ingredients onto a sheet of tin foil and scrunch together at the top to keep the juices in

Put the foil parcel on the BBQ for 10 minutes and pour over the chicken to serve

Top Tips

Be sure the chicken is cooked all the way through and no blood is on the bones. The cuts to the raw carcass help the heat penetrate during the cooking process

If it's not BBQ weather you can use the oven. First sear the chickens in a pan for 3-4 minutes on each side and finish them in an oven pre-heated to 200°c for 25 minutes or until cooked through, adding the chorizo parcels for the final ten minutes

Fish & chips with scallop potato Serves 2

Ingredients

6 200g fillets fresh cod or haddock fillets

60g self raising flour

3 lemons, halved

Salt and pepper

Chips

1kg Spunta or Maris Piper potatoes

Sunflower oil (for deep-frying)

Salt

Batter

1 pint Thornbridge beer

300g self raising flour

Salt

Tartare Sauce

250g mayonnaise

55g gherkins, roughly chopped

55g capers, roughly chopped

1 hard-boiled egg, peeled and crushed

1 lemon, zested and juiced

Salt and pepper

Small bunch flat leaf parsley, finely chopped

Scallop Potato

2 large Maris Piper potatoes, cut lengthways
1cm thick

Method

Pre-heat the deep fat fryer to 190°c and the oven
to 210°c

For the batter

To make the batter add all three ingredients
together and whisk well until smooth, then put
aside

For the tartare sauce

Combine the ingredients to your taste, place in
small pots and put aside

For the scallop potato

Put the sliced potato in a pan and cover with water
Bring to the boil and simmer for 5 minutes or until
just soft, then drain and cool on kitchen paper

When you're almost ready to eat, dip them in the
seasoned flour, then into the batter mixture and
deep fry until golden

For the chips

Peel the potatoes and cut into chips 1 centimetre
thick

Rinse well in cold water to remove the starch, then
dry on a clean tea towel

Heat the oil in a deep fat fryer to 130°c, place the
chips in the fryer basket and cook for about
5 minutes or until the chip is cooked but hasn't
coloured

Take the chips out of the basket and remove any
excess oil on a tea towel and put to one side until
needed

To finish, raise the oil temp to 190°c and place the
chips back in the basket for about 2 minutes until
crisp and golden in colour. Drain, add a little salt
and serve

For the fish

Place the self raising flour, salt and pepper into a
container big enough to fit the fish in

Dip each fillet fish in the seasoned flour mix, then
the batter and deep fry until golden. Drain on
kitchen paper and season with salt

Place a frying pan on a medium heat with a drop of
olive oil

Top and tail the lemons, cut them in half and add
them to the pan flesh-side down. Brown for 3-5
minutes

Top Tip

*When dropping the coated fish into the fryer, hold
on to the tail end for 15 seconds until a few bubbles
appear. This way the fish will swim, not sink*

What we drank ...

The invigorating carbonation and fresh nuttiness of Schneider Weisse Tap 7 Original was perfect with the avocado and crab, however Thornbridge Hopton brought a light citrusy contrast that refreshed perfectly.

Steak & Thornbridge ale pie Serves 5

Ingredients

Filling

1kg beef chuck (ask your butcher to dice into 1 inch squares)

25g plain flour, seasoned with
1 tablespoon salt and
1 tablespoon pepper

435g onions, peeled and diced

15g garlic, peeled and crushed

20ml sunflower oil

125g carrots, peeled and diced

75g celery

2 sprigs thyme

Salt and pepper

150ml Thornbridge Lord Marples ale

25ml Henderson's Relish

Chicken stock to cover

20g gravy granules

1 tablespoon brown sauce

Suet Pastry

200g plain flour

200g self raising flour

65g suet

65g butter, cubed

Cold water

Salt

Third of a tablespoon thyme, finely chopped

65g cheddar cheese

1 teaspoon grain mustard

Half teaspoon English mustard

Method

For the filling

Measure all your ingredients and pre-heat the oven to 210°c

Put a large non-stick pan on a medium heat to warm

Coat the diced beef in the seasoned flour and gently tap off the excess

Pour some of the sunflower oil into the pan then add the flour-coated beef (you may need to do this in batches). Keep turning it until the meat is a golden colour then de-glaze the pan with half of the beer

Repeat this until you have done all the meat then put it all into a large heavy-bottomed pan

Add the onions, garlic, carrots, celery and thyme and season with salt and pepper

Add the beer. If the meat isn't covered add to the liquid with chicken stock – you may not need it all

Bring to the boil and simmer for 2 hours, keeping an eye on it so it doesn't boil dry

For the pastry

Put the flours, salt and butter into a bowl and mix together using your hands until it looks like breadcrumbs. Add everything (except the water) and keep mixing before slowly adding the water until the mix forms a soft dough

Completely cover the pastry in cling film and place in the fridge for an hour. When chilled, roll the pastry out to half a centimetre thick. Use the pie dish (a small one each, or a large one for everyone) as a base and cut around the pastry. Place it on a tray and pop it back in the fridge until later

Assembly

Check to see if the meat is tender – it may need longer – then add the Henderson's Relish, brown sauce and gravy granules. Check the meat again (it should break apart easily) and taste for seasoning

When happy with the taste fill the dish and roll the pastry to 1 centimetre thick before covering the pie filling with it

Put into the oven and bake until the pasty is golden brown and the filling is hot

Have a pint too!

Top Tips

A nice touch is to retain a little of the cooking juices and serve on the side, along with some honey-roast carrots and crushed peas

Desiree and Limestone potatoes are good for mashing

What we drank ...

A classic British recipe with an archetypal bitter, the rich bittersweet nature of Thornbridge Lord Marples or robust crusty character of Acorn Barnsley Bitter fit the bill perfectly.

Lamb shank shepherd's pie **Serves 8**

Ingredients

Filling

130g carrots, peeled and diced

200g celeriac, peeled and diced

200g onions, peeled and diced

100ml olive oil

6 lamb shanks (save the bones)

Salt and pepper

500g good quality lamb mince

1 bulb garlic

1 and a half litres good quality lamb stock

3 sprigs thyme

2 sprigs rosemary

1 bay leaf

100ml balsamic vinegar

Mash

1.5kg potatoes

2 cloves garlic, peeled and crushed

50ml milk

50ml double cream

25g butter

Salt and pepper

Method

Pre-heat the oven to 180°c

For the mash

Peel and quarter the potatoes and place in a pan, cover with water and add a teaspoon of salt

When the potato is cooked drain well. Add the cream, milk, butter, salt, pepper and crushed garlic to a pan, bring to the boil and simmer until the mixture thickens

Mash the potatoes until smooth and add the cream mixture to it. Taste and season accordingly, then put to one side

For the filling

Put a third of the olive oil in an oven tray, season the lamb shanks with salt and pepper as you go and brown them in the tray on all sides

Using the same tray for flavour, add another third of the olive oil and the lamb mince and do the same. When coloured drain in a colander and put to one side

Add the last of the olive oil and all the vegetables to the same pan and brown them gently

Pour the vinegar over the vegetables and reduce by half in volume over a high heat

Place the mince and shanks into the tray with the vegetables and add the garlic, stock, thyme, rosemary and bay and bring to the boil

Cover the roasting tray with tin foil and place it in the oven for 2 and a half hours or until the bone in the lamb shanks pulls out easily. Taste the mix and correct the seasoning accordingly

When cooked, take the tray out and turn the oven up to 210°c

Pull all of the meat off the bones into strands, making sure there are no bones or sinew left in and remove the herb stalks and garlic. Keep the main lamb shank bone for presentation

Shred the lamb into the presentation dish, cover with the mince mixture and top with mash. Place the pie in the oven and cook until golden brown for 25-30 minutes

Check that the filling is hot in the middle

Serve and enjoy!

Top Tips

A nice touch is to retain a little of the cooking juices and serve on the side, along with some honey-roast carrots and crushed peas

Desiree and Limestone potatoes are good for mashing

What we drank ...

The fruity and subtly roasted flavours of a mild like Thornbridge Black Harry or Moorhouses Black Cat accentuate lamb mince as the creamy texture of the beer and mash combine.

Millionaire's shortbread

Ingredients

Base

120g butter

230g plain flour

Salt

Half a vanilla pod, de-seeded

75g caster sugar

Caramel

100g butter

100g demerara sugar

2 397g tins condensed milk

Topping

350g dark chocolate

50g white chocolate

What we drank ...

Ideally matched with the easy-drinking nuttiness of Thornbridge Sequoia or lusciously deep caramel and chocolate flavours of Nøgne-Ø Imperial Brown Ale.

Method

Pre-heat the oven to 180°c

For the shortbread

Beat the butter and sugar together until smooth and pale

Add a pinch of salt and the vanilla then fold in the flour gently until a dough is formed

Push the mixture into an 18 centimetre square baking tray using the back of a spoon and flatten evenly

Put the tray in the oven for 20 minutes or until golden brown in colour

For the filling

Place the butter, sugar and condensed milk into a heavy-bottomed saucepan and heat gently until the sugar has dissolved

Turn up the heat and keep stirring at all times until the colour becomes a light brown, then turn down the heat, simmer until the mixture thickens and has a fudge-like consistency

Pour over the cooked shortbread in the tray, then leave to cool

For the topping

Put the dark chocolate in a bowl in the microwave in 10 second bursts, or in a bowl over a pan of warm water until it has completely melted, then pour onto the set caramel

Melt the white chocolate in the same way and then spoon it in even lines on top of the dark chocolate. Using the point of a knife draw it through the chocolate in different directions to create the desired pattern

Leave to set on a worktop

Loosen the edges of the mould with a hot knife and tip out and cut into portions – or just dig in!

Top Tip

When melting chocolate over a bowl of water, be careful never to let any water touch the chocolate as it will thicken instantly

Peanut cookies   **Makes roughly 20 cookies**

Ingredients

50g salted peanuts

150g unsalted butter, softened

100g crunchy peanut butter

100g caster sugar

100g demerara sugar

250g plain flour

Method

This recipe requires time for the dough to chill

Cream together both of the sugars, butter and peanut butter together to form a smooth paste

Add in the flour a little at a time and gently mix to form a soft dough

Stir in the peanuts

Roll the dough into a sausage shape to the desired width, wrap in cling film and place in the fridge to set for 2 hours

Take the dough out of the fridge, set the oven to 180°c and line a tray with baking paper

Remove the cling film and slice the cookies 1 centimetre thick then place them on the tray with space between to allow them to spread

Put the tray into the oven and cook for 15 minutes or until golden

Remove from the oven and let them set on the tray for a couple of minutes before removing and leaving on a wire rack to cool

Dust with icing sugar and eat

What we drank ...

Thornbridge Saint Petersburg may seem an unusual match but the peanut and demerara sugar flavours are echoed by this sumptuous beer, while St. Austell HSD has a fruity and nutty caramel character that works well too.

Treacle tart Serves up to 12 (depending on how generous your slices are)

Ingredients

Filling

400g golden syrup

135g fresh breadcrumbs (no crusts!)

2 eggs

200ml double cream

Pastry

85g butter, softened

65g icing sugar

165g plain flour

1 and a half egg yolks

Pinch salt

Half tablespoon cold water

What we drank ▾▾▾

We thought the supremely sweet tart needed a contrasting character and Thornbridge Raven's clean hoppy bitterness was just the job. The tart fruit and liquorice nature of Abbot Reserve would also work well.

Method

This recipe requires time for the pastry to chill

For the pastry

Place the butter, salt and icing sugar in a food processor. Pulse until creamed together

Add the flour, water and eggs and pulse again until the mix just starts to come together

Gently knead then roll to form a long sausage shape. Wrap in cling film and place in the fridge for a couple of hours

Turn the oven on to 190°c

For the filling

Gently warm the golden syrup and cream together in a pan (be careful not to boil or it will burn)

Add the breadcrumbs to a food processor and pulse until fine, then add the eggs and syrup mix. Pulse again until smooth

Push the mix through a fine sieve and put to one side

Roll the pastry out to 2 millimetres thick until you can fill the tart case with some overhanging the edges

Use a fork to make a few holes in the bottom of the tart then line with three layers of cling film. Fill with baking beans to the top and place back in the fridge for 30 minutes

Remove the tart base and put it straight into the oven. Cook for 10-15 minutes until the edges start to colour

Turn the oven down to 160°c and cook for a further 10 minutes. Take the beans out – the pastry should be crispy on the bottom. If not pop back into the oven until it is (without the beans)

Next, brush a little of the treacle tart mix around the tart case as soon as it comes out of the oven. This will help to seal the cooked pastry

Turn the oven down to 140°c

Fill the base to the top with the syrup mixture then slowly slide the tart back into the oven and cook for 40 minutes or until the tart has just set

Once out of the oven allow to cool and with a very sharp knife cut the overlapping pastry away from the tart

Serve with clotted cream

Sticky toffee pudding Serves roughly 10

Ingredients

350g sugar

110g butter

350g self raising flour

350g dates

4 eggs

1 pint water

2 tablespoons bicarbonate of soda

1 teaspoon mixed spice

Method

Pre-heat the oven to 130˚c

Cream the butter and sugar until pale

Mix in the eggs then fold in the flour and mixed spice

Cook the dates in the water with the Bicarbonate of Soda until soft then smash with a whisk

Add the date mixture to the rest of the ingredients and mix well

Line a 25 centimetre baking tin with parchment paper and bake for 1 hour or until cooked

What we drank ...

Sweet and sticky, this pudding needs the crisp clean refreshment of Thornbridge Kill Your Darlings or grassy bitterness Hobson's Best Bitter to cleanse and re-set the taste buds for another mouthful.

Thornbridge Saint Petersburg ice cream

Ingredients

Caramel

200g caster sugar

50ml Thornbridge Saint Petersburg stout

Ice Cream

300ml milk

300ml cream

90g egg yolk

100g caster sugar

Beer Reduction

150ml of Thornbridge Saint Petersburg stout

What we drank ...

Well worth the effort, this deliciously sweet yet curiously roasted ice cream allows the nut and honey aromas of Thornbridge Bracia or chocolate and coffee taste of Brooklyn Chocolate Stout to shine.

Method

For the caramel

Put the sugar in a heavy-bottomed saucepan then add the 50ml of stout

Bring to the boil and continue cooking on a medium heat until it starts to turn into a light caramel

Do not shake or touch the pan – this will crystalise the caramel and it won't work

Leave it in the pan and put to one side

For the ice cream

Bring the milk to the boil

Whisk the egg yolk and sugar together. Temper the yolks by adding the milk a little at a time to prevent curdling

Pour the mixture into a clean pan and put back on the heat stirring constantly, until the mixture will coat the back of a wooden spoon

Remove from the heat and start to cool as quickly as possible (putting the mixture in a bowl over a bowl of iced water does the trick)

For the beer reduction

Take the 150ml of stout, pour it into a pan and bring to the boil. Continue boiling until you are left with about half the mixture

Add the reduction to the caramel, which should still be warm

Add this mixture to the ice cream and push through a sieve to remove any lumps

Churn in an ice cream maker and place in the freezer

Top Tips

Be careful when making the caramel – the temperature gets incredibly hot

Do not overcook the eggs or you will end up with them scrambled

An ice cream maker is a must-have

THORNBRIDGE HALL

GARDENS

Down at the bottom of the garden...

Thornbridge Hall – we had to come back to where it all began. The wonderful, fresh produce grown in the grounds by our gardeners and the wild boars that roam in the woodland lend themselves perfectly to this chapter.

The whole estate is about 100 acres of properly laid out parkland with astounding views of the Peak District National Park, 10 of which are formal gardens that were laid out well over a century ago. They were part of George Marples' vision to create '1,000 shades of green', which he wanted to be able to view from his bedroom window.

Our head gardener, Brian de Wynter, has worked on the estate for over a decade and, along with his team, has developed the gardens into the thriving hubbub of colour and scent they are today. There's a central orangery flanked by hothouses and greenhouses set in the footprint of the original Victorian glasshouse – it's a picturesque, serene setting.

The defunct tennis courts, replaced by flower and vegetable beds, add to the yield of fresh produce and many of the herbs and plants grown here are used by the brewers in some of our more esoteric beers – it's great how well they work in harmony.

The Wild Boar Man

Alongside our fruit and veg come the wild boars. Not many people around Bakewell know the name Tom Clarke – but mention The Wild Boar Man and you'll often see a flash of recognition.

Tom's love of the local woods and streams stems from his childhood, spent mainly in such places in preference to the classroom. Following his heart, he knew that he would eventually make his living off the land and so it came to be, following training as a butcher at Chatsworth and a stint on a New Zealand farm.

With our full support, Tom introduced his first group of wild boars to the 20 acres of woodland around the Hall in 2007. He works alone, farming, butchering and selling the meat, which has enabled him to increase the herd from 10 to about 50. He now supplies the Hall and our pubs and restaurants, as well as shops and other local boozers.

His wild boars are the only ones in the country to be reared in the woods and have the mashings from the brewery mixed into their feed – a factor which benefits their unique taste.

All these elements combined to form a great day spent cooking, eating and drinking at Thornbridge. It was a delight to sit back and savour all the things our fantastic staff work so hard to create year-round and a great reminder of what a privilege it is to live and work in the Peak District National Park.

– Jim Harrison

THORNBRIDGE WILD BOARS

The wild boars at Thornbridge are fed twice a day, seven days a week on a mixture of feed, beer mashings and pine cones.

Most are reared for 18 months, at which time they are perfect for roasting, sausages and smoked cuts.

The chefs at Thornbridge have fed them various things to enhance their flavour – grapefruit and pink peppercorns were snorted at, while blackberries got a slightly better reception.

The beer won out though – they clearly have excellent taste.

Bacon, Isle of Mull cheddar & Thornbridge beer bread

Makes roughly 30 small rolls

Ingredients

Bread

500g granary flour

500g white bread flour

10g salt

50g fresh bakers' yeast

200ml Thornbridge Kipling ale, plus a little for brushing

350ml water

140g smoked bacon, diced and cooked

100g Isle of Mull cheddar cheese, finely grated

Glaze

250ml Thornbridge Kipling ale

50g sugar

Method

For the bread

Mix both the flours and yeast in a bowl

Add the beer and water and bring together

Cover with a wet cloth and leave to prove somewhere warm until it doubles in size

Cut the dough in half and roll it out into a rectangle 5 millimetres thick

Add the cheese, bacon and salt and knead

Brush the rectangle with beer and roll to make a 'Swiss roll' effect

Cut the roll into portions 3 centimetres thick and place them on grease proof paper on a tray

Now prove again for about 30 minutes somewhere warm until doubled in size again

Pre-heat the oven to 210°c

When the bread has proved, put the trays into the oven and cook for roughly 10 minutes or until golden brown (when tapped on the bottom the bread should sound hollow)

Turn the rolls out of the trays and sit them on a wire rack until cool

For the glaze

Pour the remaining beer into a pan with the sugar and reduce it on a medium heat until a syrup is formed

Brush the glaze over the rolls

Warm the bread in the oven for a couple of minutes before eating

Top Tip

Never let the yeast touch the salt – or it will reach an untimely end!

What we drank ...

The mellow nature of Thornbridge Lord Marples malt echoes that of the toasted rolls and provides the perfect background for the smoked bacon and cheese. Hawkshead Bitter would be a great match too.

Cheese board & homemade chutney

Ingredients

Cheeses we used

Cerney Pyramid

Lincolnshire Poacher

Barncliffe Brie

Yorkshire Blue

Yorkshire Fine Fettle

Cropwell Bishop Stilton

Basic Chutney

355ml cider vinegar

130g caster sugar

680g Bramley apples peeled, cored and diced

160g onions, diced

70g sultanas

1 lemon, zested

30g fresh ginger, grated

Half cinnamon stick

Pinch salt

10g mixed spice

5g red chilli, seeded and finely chopped

100g ripe pears, peeled, cored and diced

200ml water

Method

Place all of the ingredients into a heavy-bottomed pan

Bring the contents to the boil and turn down to a simmer until most of the liquid has evaporated – the mixture should look like it has started to thicken

Ladle the mixture into sterilised jars, leave it to cool and store in the fridge until required

Top Tips

Make sure the cheese is served room temperature – you will see what a difference it makes to the flavour

We served our cheese with red wine jelly, quince jelly, homemade breads, homemade chutney and grapes

What we drank ...

A cheeseboard is the perfect opportunity to experiment with a range of beers to experience delicious complementary and contrasting options. From Thornbridge we enjoyed the spiciness of Jaipur, richness and depth of Saint Petersburg and nutty toffee flavours of Kill Your Darlings. You may also enjoy Young's Special London Ale, Hobson's Postmans' Knock and Hepworth Blonde organic lager.

Broad bean, pea, mint & feta salad

Ingredients

100g broad beans, shelled

100g peas, shelled

75g good quality Greek Feta cheese

Small bunch fresh mint

Extra Virgin Olive oil (to dress)

Salt and freshly ground black pepper

Method

Place a pan of water on the stove, add a pinch of salt and bring to the boil

Prepare a bowl of water, half filled with ice

Add the broad beans, then the peas to the boiling water and cook until tender, then refresh in the iced water

When the peas and beans are ice cold drain in a colander

Crumble the feta into a bowl, add the beans and peas, pour a little olive oil over and season with salt and pepper

Wash the mint, slice finely then and add to the mixture

Toss the salad gently, taste and serve

What we drank ...

We thought the fresh pine aromas of Thornbridge Chiron blended with the mint, peas and beans, while the crisp bitterness cut through the salty feta. This would alternatively match with the great American flavours of Sierra Nevada Pale Ale.

Roast Thornbridge garden vegetables with Manuka honey Serves 4

Ingredients

50g Manuka honey (other good quality honey can be used)

40ml extra virgin olive oil

1 carrot, peeled and sliced at an angle 1cm thick

1 courgette, peeled and sliced at an angle 1cm thick

1 red onion, peeled and quartered

3 whole beetroots

Half a leek

2 sprigs thyme

1 sprig rosemary

1 garlic bulb, halved sideways

2 baby fennel, each cut into 8

1 banana shallot, peeled and halved (small onions are a good substitute)

Salt and pepper

Top Tips

All our veg came from the Thornbridge Hall gardens on the day we cooked it

Roasting vegetables individually to begin with will ensure they are all served perfectly cooked

Method

Set the oven to 200°c

Put the carrots and fennel in a bowl with a teaspoon of oil. Season with salt and pepper and mix well then roast in the oven for 6 minutes

Prepare the onions, shallots and beetroot in the same way and roast together on a tray for 4 minutes

Cut the leek in the same way as the carrots then cook in a pan of boiling salted water for 2 minutes. Drain and put to one side

Put the garlic on a small roasting tray, add a drop of the olive oil and roast until it starts to colour

Put all the ingredients on one large roasting tray and gently toss them together using your hands. Squeeze the garlic cloves out of the bulb

Season with salt and pepper and add the rosemary, thyme and honey

Place the tray in the oven for 10-12 minutes until all the vegetables are cooked

Taste for seasoning and serve

What we drank ...

Roasting brings out the full sweetness and flavour of the fresh garden vegetables and we thought the smooth maltiness, light body and fruity spices of Thornbridge Versa enhanced those flavours, while the gently caramelised roast nature of Bernard Dark made an excellent combination.

The 'Chiefs' and Smithy

Marco Caires, Jack Baker, Les Rennie & Richard Smith

Wild boar & borlotti bean stew Serves 4

Ingredients

1.375kg diced wild boar shoulder

175g Spanish onions, peeled and finely chopped

35ml olive oil

Quarter of a bulb of garlic, peeled and finely chopped

225g carrots, peeled and sliced at an angle

1 and a half sticks of celery, sliced at an angle

Half a red chilli, finely chopped

50g tomato purée

2 tablespoons smoked paprika

1 red pepper, seeded and roughly chopped

200g borlotti beans

2 and a half tins chopped tomatoes

350g new potatoes

350g chorizo sausage links, peeled and sliced 1cm thick

250ml Thornbridge Sequoia beer

Water to cover the boar generously

Salt and pepper

Method

Put the boar in a large pan and cover with water. Bring to the boil and remove any excess fat that comes to the top. Simmer for 20 minutes

In another pan warm the oil gently, add the garlic and once you can smell the aroma add the onions

Cook the onions until soft and colourless, then add the smoked paprika and cook for a further minute

Add the tomato purée and chilli

Ladle 1 pint of the boar stock into the tomato mixture to create a sauce-like consistency

Add the carrots, celery and tinned tomatoes, bring back to the boil and turn down to simmer for 10 minutes

Add generous pinches of salt and pepper then the Thornbridge Sequoia beer and chorizo

Remove the excess fat from the boar pan again and strain the meat through a colander. Keep the liquid for later

Add the boar to the other pan and slowly add two pints cooking liquid until a sauce-like consistency is achieved

Keep the stew simmering for a further 30 minutes

Add the new potatoes and cook for another 45 minutes

To check if the meat is ready, take a piece from the pan and taste or cut it with a knife. If there is a lot of resistance it may need up to another

90 minutes cooking time. If it seems a little softer add the red peppers and simmer for another 15 minutes

Add the borlotti beans and taste for seasoning

Check the meat and the new potatoes – they should be soft but still hold their shape

Serve in a warm bowl with crusty bread

Top Tips

A good substitute for boar is rare breed pork

The keys to this dish are building the layers of flavour as you go and tasting throughout

This stew tastes great the next day too. It will have set slightly, so to serve warm it very slowly until it's piping hot

What we drank ...

The full, rich and complex flavours of Thornbridge Evenlode or Tracquair Jacobite ale are a great match for the depth of savoury character of the boar, spice of the sauce and nuttiness of the borlotti beans.

INNOVATION · PASSION · KNOWLEDGE

Thornbridge

EVENLODE

BROWN PORTER
6.2% ABV

Eccles cakes with Lancashire cheese

Ingredients

Eccles Cakes

500g currants

100g sultanas

200g Muscovado sugar

1 teaspoon ground allspice

Pinch of nutmeg

2 lemons, zested

2 oranges, zested

75g warm golden syrup

700g puff pastry

Glaze

Egg white (for brushing)

Caster sugar (for sprinkling)

10 slices Lancashire cheese

What we drank ...

The sweet richness of Thornbridge Bracia goes well with the vine fruits and the dry roasted finish cuts through the cheese while accentuating its acidity and highlighting the nutty notes of the beer. The sweet, yet roasted notes of Westmalle 10 would also be a great match for this combination.

Method

The first stage of this recipe requires preparation the day before

Mix together all the Eccles Cake ingredients until smooth and leave to set in the fridge overnight

When you're ready to bake, pre-heat the oven to 200°c

Roll out the puff pastry to 3 millimetres thick and cut into circles roughly 5 inches wide, discarding the trimmings

Place a good dollop of the mixture in the centre of each circle leaving a 1 centimetre gap around the edge

Brush a thin layer of egg white around the edge then fold the pastry over 8 times in a crimping motion to form a circle, then seal

Flatten each cake between the palms of your hands

Make 3 slits in the centre of each cake and place on a baking tray. Glaze with egg white and sprinkle generously with sugar

Cook for 15 minutes or until golden

Add the cheese on top and serve

Top Tips

Lancashire tastes great with Eccles Cakes, but you can serve them with any cheese you like. Blue cheeses taste great too

The slashes in Eccles Cakes are said to represent the Holy Trinity

RECIPES FROM OUR
FRIENDS

With family and friends at the heart of what we do we invited some of those we've met along the way to contribute a recipe and beer pairing of their own.

Cooking and photographing the following dishes submitted by our friends was a special way to conclude our recipes.

We hope you enjoy them as much as we did...

Sticky BBQ ribs with Alaskan smoked porter Serves 4-6

by Ben McFarland, award-winning beer writer

Ingredients

Basic Rub

4 whole pork baby back ribs

1 sprig rosemary

1 sprig thyme

15g salt

5g fennel seeds

10g paprika

5g cayenne pepper

5g chilli powder

2 cloves

Quarter teaspoon cumin seeds

Quarter teaspoon black peppercorns

3 cloves garlic

125ml bourbon

BBQ Basting Sauce

500g tomato purée

65g honey

75ml cider vinegar

75g brown sugar

5ml balsamic vinegar

15ml Henderson's Relish

5ml Tabasco

2 cloves garlic, thinly sliced (ideally with a razor like in Goodfellas)

Quarter teaspoon sea salt

10ml golden rum (I like Angostura 1919)

Method

This recipe requires time to slow-cook the ribs

For the basic rub

In a pestle and mortar grind the salt, fennel seeds, paprika, cayenne pepper, chilli powder, cloves, cumin seeds and black peppercorns for 2-3 minutes

Add the garlic and grind again

For the ribs

Stab each rib around 10 times with a fork

Rub in the spice mix with the bourbon, thyme and rosemary, massaging each rib for 1-2 minutes

Leave to rest for an hour

When the hour's up pre-heat the oven to 150°c and cook for 3 and a half hours

For the basting sauce

While the ribs are cooking, prepare the basting sauce

Put all the ingredients into a bowl and mix well

Taste and, if required, add in some chopped chillies (the heat will mellow on the BBQ)

Once the rib cooking time is up, coat them generously in the sauce

Make sure the BBQ isn't blazing hot, then lay the ribs evenly across the grill

When the sauce starts sizzling flip them over and baste with more sauce

Repeat so that they become sticky

Serve with a jacket potato and chunky coleslaw

Super smoky Rauchbiers from the German town of Bamberg, such as Aecht Schlenkerla Rauchbier can be pretty heavy-handed. For a little less smoke but with enough sweetness to mirror ribs' marinade or glaze, reach for Alaskan Smoked Porter.

To drink: Alaskan Smoked Porter, 6.5%

From the last frontier, first brewed 25 years ago and released every November, this North American Rauchbier is inspired by turn-of-the-century Alaskan ale-makers who malted their own barley and smoked it over indigenous alder wood.

Brewed using glacial water sourced from the Juneau Ice Field spanning 1,500 miles, it's brought back a lot of bling from the Great American Beer Festival, having won 11 medals since 1988.

It's a strapping, seductive and unashamedly masculine beer that matures magnificently in the cellar where Father Time lengthens out the complexity. Mellowed out by other malts, the smoke is not stifling like its Bamberg brethren and the alder wood embers drift deliciously away on the palate.

The pairing avoids being stiflingly smoky by the sweetness of the sticky ribs' sauce.

Best drunk in the Alaskan wilderness after a hard day killing elk with one's bare hands, going toe-to-toe with grizzlies and washing moose kill from the back of your pick-up.

– Ben McFarland

www.thinkingdrinkers.com
@thinkingdrinks

Pork Skyfall Serves 1

by Olly Smith, TV presenter, wine expert, foodie and writer

I named this recipe 'Pork Skyfall' because I put it together on a night I had pork planned for dinner and because I was excited about the release of the Bond film!

This dish is easy and quick, so it's a perfect sweet and spicy weeknight treat and marvellous with a sip of hoppy craft beer. I served mine with a side salad of fresh spinach leaves, crumbled stilton and small diced chunks of fresh mango.

To drink: Rocky Head Pale Ale or Thornbridge Chiron

Pairing drinks and dishes is about having fun – the rule of thumb is that if you like it then it's a great match. But if you fancy giving a bit of thought as to whether you want to balance or contrast your drink with your dish, you can begin to explore the different dimensions of flavour, texture and intensity and how they affect your palate.

A bit of spice in a dish works a treat with a good dose of fruity flavour in the accompanying drink and the sweetness in my Pork Skyfall also flourishes with a decent boost of richness in the glass.

For me, a kick of warming spice on the plate works a treat with a cool pale ale and whether it's a takeaway curry or something more fancy, Rocky Head Pale Ale rocks my socks for its exuberance and lip-smacking hoppy tang. Thornbridge's Chiron also does the trick. Boom!

Ingredients

1 pork fillet	Soy sauce
Salt	Sweet chilli sauce
Sesame oil	200g rice
Sunflower oil	400ml water

Method

Seal the pork fillet in an ovenproof frying pan with half sesame oil and half sunflower oil

Season with salt and brown each side of the fillet

After 4-5 minutes transfer the whole pan with the pork and juices to a hot oven, around 180-200°c

Bring the water to the boil with a good pinch of salt, then add the rice and boil for 5 minutes

Take off the heat and sip your beer while the rice cooks in the steam for 15 minutes

Take the pan out of the oven (use oven gloves or your hand will ignite)

Splash a bit of soy sauce over the pork fillet then smother it in sweet chilli sauce in the pan and allow to reduce for another minute while spooning it over the meat

Take the pork out of the pan and leave to rest

Have a few more sips of beer

Carve the fillet into large triangular chunky pieces to show the juicy meat and glazed outside and serve on top of the rice in hearty bowls

Sip more beer, relax and put your feet up

Over and out!

- Olly Smith

www.ollysmith.com
@jollyolly

Wild Swan, chicken, leek, ham & Cornish brie Serves 4-6

by Melissa Cole, beer writer, sommALEier and author of *Let Me Tell You About Beer*

Ingredients

Shortcrust Pastry

Egg (for brushing)

500g plain flour (plus some extra for rolling)

125g unsalted butter (plus extra to grease dish)

125g lard

pinch salt

1 teaspoon cider vinegar

1 egg, beaten

Cold water

Filling

500g skinless, boneless chicken thighs

25g plain flour, seasoned with 1 tablespoon of salt and 1 tablespoon of pepper

100g diced prosciutto

340g white onion, finely chopped

2 garlic cloves, finely chopped

260g leeks, cut into discs

200ml chicken gravy

250ml Thornbridge Wild Swan (and more to drink with it!)

1 tablespoon dried tarragon

100g Cornish brie (I use Llawnroc)

Salt and pepper

Groundnut oil

Method

For the pastry

Sift flour and salt into a large mixing bowl

Rub the butter and lard into the flour until it resembles breadcrumbs

Add vinegar and enough cold water to bring the mixture together into a smooth dough

Wrap in cling film, chill in the fridge for 30 minutes

For the filling

Warm a pan on a medium to high heat

Chop the chicken thighs into bite-sized chunks and toss in seasoned flour

Put oil in the pan and add the chicken

When it's golden brown on one side, turn over and throw in the onion and prosciutto

When the chicken is golden brown all over, the onions should be softened and the prosciutto should be golden and crispy

Add in all the vegetables

Throw in your beer to deglaze the pan then reduce

Add garlic and leeks and cook for a minute

Add the chicken stock then gently reduce again. It will take about 20-30 minutes to reduce to a thickish sauce. Put in the fridge to cool

Assemble your pie

Pre-heat the oven to 180°c

Roll out the pastry to fill your pie dish and make enough for a lid

Carefully place it in a suitable, lightly-buttered dish and leave some hanging over sides. Leave to rest in the fridge for 30 minutes

Fill the dish with baking parchment (quick tip, scrunch up your baking parchment before trying to fit it in, makes it easier – as well as a satisfying noise) and fill with baking beans or rice

Blind-bake for 15 minutes or until the pastry is just beginning to colour

Once it's set, remove the baking beans and parchment, allow to cool for 10-15 minutes then trim the excess off the sides

Put half your cooled filling in the pie, stud with torn-off chunks of half your brie and repeat the process with the rest of your filling and cheese

Put the pastry top on, crimping it to the base as you go. Poke a hole in the middle to let the steam out and coat with egg wash

Turn the oven up to 200°c for about 25 minutes or until the top is golden and the insides bubbling!

— Melissa Cole

www.letmetellyouaboutbeer.co.uk
@melissacole

I don't know about you, but anything with the word pie in the title is enough to catch my attention.

This is my take on a chicken and ham pie — a filling I always find disappointing as it's generally claggy and bland. I wanted to make an updated version that has a little more to it and I think I've succeeded.

You don't need much more to accompany it than some greens (I like samphire and peas) and carrots.

To drink: Thornbridge Wild Swan

Thornbridge Wild Swan goes gloriously with this, as does Hop Back Brewery's Summer Lightning — really any spritzy, citrusy blonde ale will go well. I also think that the Saison Dupont is a good accompaniment too, so the choice is yours.

Crab cakes 'Garrett' Serves 4

by Garrett Oliver, Brewmaster of The Brooklyn Brewery, author of The Brewmaster's Table and Editor-in-Chief of The Oxford Companion to Beer

This is one of my favorite recipes. I have cooked this in front of audiences many times – most recently in London for a few hundred people at Whole Foods. The recipe was also published in The New York Times back in 2004. I serve this with a diced avocado and tomato salad, dressed with olive oil, balsamic and a wedge of lime

To drink: Thornbridge Jaipur or Brooklyn Brewery's East India Pale Ale

These crab cakes are great with India pale ales. The citrusy character of the hops in Jaipur picks up on the lime juice in the crab cakes and the flavours of coriander leaf – it's a perfect combination.

Ingredients

450g lump crab meat (or good quality picked crab)

150g panko breadcrumbs

Small bunch coriander, coarsely chopped

1-2 small jalapenos, to taste

1 yellow pepper, finely diced

1 large egg

150g mayonnaise

110g red onion, finely diced

1 heaped teaspoon Madras curry powder

1 heaped teaspoon cumin powder

1 lime, juiced

10g fresh ginger, grated

Vegetable oil

Salt

Method

Pre-heat the oven to 190°c

In a bowl add the red onion, yellow pepper, jalapenos, coriander and crab meat

In another bowl whisk the egg and add the mayonnaise until smooth

Squeeze half the lime juice into the mayonnaise mixture with the cumin, curry powder and a pinch of salt

Add the mayonnaise mixture to the crab mixture, stirring carefully so as not to break up the crab meat

Carefully fold in 100g of panko breadcrumbs

Split the mixture into 8 cakes

Toss the cakes in the remaining breadcrumbs and sear in a hot pan of vegetable oil

When both sides are golden brown remove from the pan and place on an oven tray

Bake in the oven for around 6 minutes and serve hot

– Garrett Oliver

www.brooklynbrewery.com
@GarrettOliver

Export stout "Affogato" with vanilla ice cream

Serves as many as you make it for
by Pete Brown, award-winning beer writer

This recipe is so basic it's almost cheating. In fact I would say it definitely IS cheating were it not for the fact that I was served it in a highly reputable French brasserie in the heart of London.

To drink: Kernel London Export Stout or Brooklyn Black Chocolate Stout

It began when I was trying to convince the brasserie to let me host a beer and food matching dinner. I'd taken along a selection of bottles to demonstrate beer's variety and complexity (and drama – my bottle of Worthington White Shield spontaneously exploded while sitting on the table).

There was quite a lot of cautious nodding and then I came to my final beer – a big, chocolatey stout. "Now this," I said, "is so amazing that you could simply pour it on vanilla ice cream and serve it as a dessert."

Of course I'd forgotten that I was sitting in a brasserie, and the owner simply complied, went to fetch a bowl of vanilla ice cream and poured the beer over it. She watched the near-black beer puddle, become marbled with creamy traces and took a big scoop.

"Ok," she nodded, "You've convinced me about beer and food. How soon can we get this organised?"

Of course, I knew that I'd presented a very crude version of a dish. This was confirmed when my 'Pour Some Beer Over Some Ice Cream' appeared on the evening's menu as 'Export Stout "Affogato".' I thought it looked and tasted much better than my version, so I went home and looked up what 'affogato' was.

Here's what Wikipedia says:

An affogato (Italian, 'drowned') is a coffee-based beverage. It usually takes the form of a scoop of vanilla gelato or ice cream topped with a shot of hot espresso. Some variations also include a shot of Amaretto or other liqueur.

Turns out the chef had done nothing different from what I'd suggested after all.

Ingredients

A dark export or chocolate stout, such as Kernel London Export Stout or Brooklyn Black Chocolate Stout

Good quality vanilla ice cream

Method

Take the beer and open it

Place a scoop of ice cream in a small, round bowl

Pour the beer over the ice cream. Or, if feeling posh, serve the beer in a small jug on the side

So ridiculously simple. So devastatingly effective

– Pete Brown

petebrown.blogspot.co.uk
@PeteBrownBeer

Banana bread pudding drizzled with hot caramel sauce

Serves up to 12
by Marverine Cole, beer sommelier and writer

Ingredients

Banana Bread Pudding

570g day-old bread

450ml warm milk

70g butter

20g custard powder

3 eggs

Pinch of cinnamon

1 teaspoon vanilla essence

225g granulated sugar

2 ripe bananas

100g raisins or sultanas

Pinch nutmeg

Caramel Sauce

190g butter

250g granulated sugar

120ml double cream (make sure it's slightly warmed up)

1 tablespoon vanilla essence

Method

For the pudding

Add the butter to the warm milk and whisk to melt it in

In a bowl, make a paste by mixing a few tablespoons of the warm liquid into the custard powder

Then whisk the custard mix into the rest of the milk and butter combination

Put the eggs, sugar, nutmeg, cinnamon and vanilla into a separate bowl and whisk until it becomes a cream

Whisk the egg mixture and the milk and butter combo together

Break your day old loaf up into small pieces and place in a bowl

Thinly slice the bananas and put them in the bowl with the raisins or sultanas

Pour the liquid on top and mix it up well, making sure the bread is submerged. Cover with a tea towel and leave for 15-20 minutes so the bread soaks up all the lovely liquid

Pre-heat the oven to 180°c

Put the mixture into a standard loaf tin and cook on the middle shelf for 50 minutes until a golden crust forms

Remove from the oven and leave to cool

For the caramel sauce

Slowly melt the sugar in a deep pan over a medium heat. Keep stirring for around 10 minutes until it turns golden brown

Stir in the butter

Turn the heat off and whisk cream in a little at a time

Add the vanilla

To serve, slice the loaf and a banana and caramelise both using caster sugar and a blow torch. Pour the caramel sauce over the top

– Marverine Cole

www.beerbeauty.co.uk
@BeerBeauty

I wanted to include this recipe because it's something my mum used to make for us as kids, but she hasn't done it for years – I think she reckons we've grown out of it.

At Christmas she used to throw in a little bit of Jamaican Overproof Rum (usually Wray and Nephew) if she was really being daring to give it that Caribbean Yuletide zing.

To drink: Thornbridge Versa

The lush, complementary flavours of the banana in the pudding with the lovely banana aroma and taste that come from Versa are a delight. Then the beer does a terrific job of wiping away all the lovely caramel sauce that sticks all over your mouth. Corrr!

INNOVATION. PASSION. KNOWLEDGE
THORNBRIDGE BEERS

Thornbridge Beers

At Thornbridge we take traditional styles of beer and give them our contemporary, 'never ordinary' treatment using fantastic hops, malts, herbs, spices and fruits from around the world.

With around 300 industry and consumer awards for our cask, keg and bottled beers, we believe we are leading the way for British craft beers.

Here are some of the awards our brewery has been lucky enough to win:

Black Harry

Dark, Fruity Ale, 3.9%

A fruity aroma with notes of raspberry, a light, creamy body and long nutty finish. Dark, refreshing and very drinkable.

Available in: Cask

Brother Rabbit

Crisp, Golden Ale, 4.0%

Lemon zest in colour with a clean, hoppy aroma. A resinous finish and some bitterness.

Available in: Cask

Chiron

American Pale, 5.0%

Chiron Pale Ale is golden in colour. Subtle but spicy aroma with citric notes from the hops, balanced by biscuity malt and tart citrus fruit.

Available in: Keg, Bottle

Halcyon

Imperial IPA, 7.4%

Rich fruit and hop aroma. Chewy, juicy malts and intense hoppiness with a hint of tangerine and pear drops. Ends with a well-balanced bitterness.

Available in: Keg, Bottle

Jaipur

India Pale Ale, 5.9%

A citrus-dominated IPA, soft and smooth yet builds to a crescendo of massive hoppiness accentuated by honey. An enduring, bitter finish.

Available in: Cask, Keg, Bottle

Kill Your Darlings

Vienna Style Lager, 5.0%

Reddish brown in colour, this Vienna style lager has a medium body, characterised by malty aroma and slight malt sweetness.

Available in: Keg, Bottle

Kipling

South Pacific Pale Ale, 5.2%

Golden blonde with a passion fruit, gooseberry and mango aroma. An initial sweetness and medium body are balanced by a bitter finish.

Available in: Cask, Bottle

Lord Marples

Classic Bitter, 4.0%

Surprisingly smooth with light toffee and caramel characters, a mixture of floral and spicy hop notes and a pleasing bitter finish.

Available in: Cask

Raven

Black IPA, 6.6%

The name's an oxymoron — the beer is complex and stunning. Five malts and six hops combine for bitter chocolate flavours with dark roasted fruits.

Available in: Keg, Bottle

Saint Petersburg

Imperial Russian Stout, 7.4%

Rich and dark with subtle peatiness. Molasses, liquorice and chocolate goodness in a smooth, warming liquid. Finishes with distinct bitterness.

Available in: Cask, Keg, Bottle

Sequoia

American Amber Ale, 4.5%

Beautiful citrus and pine notes. Smooth and velvety, a medium body with hints of roasted hazelnut, toffee and caramel malt flavours.

Available in: Cask

Tzara

Köln Style Beer, 4.8%

Tzara is a hybrid beer, fermented like ale but matured like a lager. A broad, almost fruity palate with some bready notes. A crisp, refreshing beer.

Available in: Keg, Bottle

Versa

Weisse Beer, 5.0%

This fresh, fruity Weisse beer pours a hazy, burnt orange and has well-balanced flavours of clove spiciness, banana and bubblegum.

Available in: Keg, Bottle

Wild Swan

White Gold Pale Ale, 3.5%

White Swan is white gold in colour with aromas of light, bitter lemon, a hint of herbs and a subtle spiciness. A great, refreshing beer.

Available in: Cask, Bottle

OUR
ESTABLISHMENTS

Artisan

www.artisansheffield.co.uk

The Bath Hotel

www.beerinthebath.co.uk

The Beauchief Restaurant & Rooms

www.thebeauchief.com

The Coach & Horses

www.mycoachandhorses.co.uk

The Cross Scythes

www.crossscythes.co.uk

The Cricket Inn

www.cricketinn.co.uk

Dada Bar

www.dadabar.co.uk

The Greystones

www.mygreystones.co.uk

Graze Inn

www.grazeinn.co.uk

The Hallamshire House

www.myhallamshire.co.uk

The Stag's Head

www.mystagshead.co.uk

The Inn at Troway

www.troway.co.uk

Relish

www.relishrelish.co.uk

Richard Smith would like to thank:

I'd personally like to thank chefs Les Rennie, Jack Baker and Marco Caires for their fantastic contribution. Without their hard work, commitment and amazing cooking skills there probably wouldn't be any food in this book!

I had some amazing days working on this – cooking with Jack in Colchester was one of the best days of my life. The day in the garden at Thornbridge with all the lads was truly special, as was our BBQ at the Cricket Inn with my wife Victoria and my boys, William and Thomas.

Thank you Les for your work on the book and all you do for the business; you are an incredibly talented chef and a true friend.

Jack, thank you for the last 10 years, you are one special guy – I could not ask for a better man to help us with all we do.

Chef Marco, you deliver the goods at the Cricket. Your passion and dedication is an inspiration and we are fortunate to have you.

Guys from the bottom of my heart thank you – the inner circle lives on!

I also want to thank Simon and Jim – great friends as well as colleagues and a pleasure to work with.

Simon Webster would like to thank:

A big thank you to our fantastic brewers: you make the great beer to accompany this great food and there wouldn't be a book if you didn't!

Jim Harrison would like to thank:

My thanks go to each and every one of the wonderful staff at Thornbridge Hall – without you it wouldn't be the place it is.

Adelle Draper would like to thank:

Les Rennie and Jack Baker for their help and patience; Alex Buchanan and Jodi Hinds for their time and input; and Lesley Draper and Steve Caddy for their suggestions and proofing. Thanks also to Simon, Jim, Richard and Victoria for letting me loose on this book.

Thanks to Jodi Hinds for really getting to know us and producing such special, atmospheric photographs that have brought our book to life.

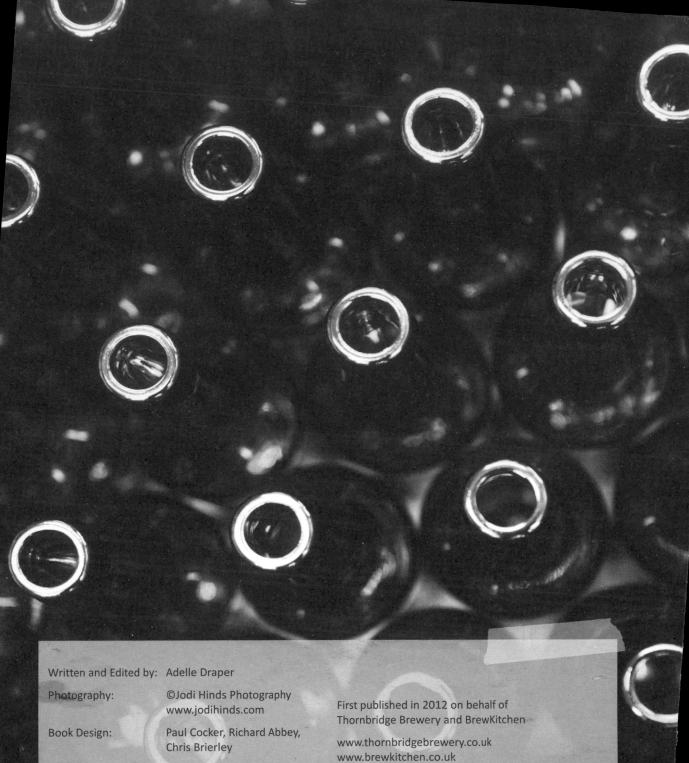

Written and Edited by: Adelle Draper

Photography: ©Jodi Hinds Photography
                         www.jodihinds.com

Book Design: Paul Cocker, Richard Abbey,
                         Chris Brierley

Cover Design: Helen Flather

Contributors: Alex Barlow, Pete Brown,
                         Marverine Cole, Melissa Cole,
                         Ben McFarland, Garrett Oliver,
                         Olly Smith

Design and Layout: ©Regional Magazine Company
                         www.rmcbooks.co.uk

First published in 2012 on behalf of
Thornbridge Brewery and BrewKitchen

www.thornbridgebrewery.co.uk
www.brewkitchen.co.uk